Punchlines

Barbara Mitchelhill

Hutchinson

London   Sydney   Auckland   Johannesburg

Contents

The Fire

4 parts:
Lisa, Pam, Baby, Man

Scene The living room of a flat.

Baby	*Cries loudly*
Lisa	Oh, do shut up Helen. I can't talk to Aunty Pam with you yelling.
Baby	*Still cries*
Pam	Put her in the bedroom. She just wants her afternoon nap, that's all.
Lisa	Good idea. I'll put her in her cot.
	[Lisa *goes out with* Baby *and the crying fades. She comes back alone*]
Pam	That's better
Lisa	I know she's noisy but I wouldn't be without her.
Pam	Yes. My kids brighten up my life.
Lisa	Do they really, Pam?

Pam	Yes. There's not one of them ever thinks of switching a light off.
Lisa	I know what you mean.
Pam	But how do you like it in the flat? I haven't seen you since you moved in. It's quiet here, isn't it?
Lisa	Yes – when Helen's asleep.
Pam	Well, I can hear something now. What is it?
Lisa	Crikey. I think it's the fire alarm.
Pam	Don't get in a flap, Lisa. I expect the kids set it off. The kids in these flats are always in trouble.
Lisa	But I can smell smoke ... I can smell smoke.
Pam	No, no ... you just think you can.
Lisa	But I can ... and I can see it, too.
Pam	Well, I can't see it. It's all in the mind ... all in the mind.
Lisa	But it's coming under the door – look.
Pam	Oh yes. [*Coughing now*] I think I can see it.
Lisa	I'm going to get Helen. We've got to get out of here.

Pam	I'll open the door. We'll go down the stairs.
	[Pam *almost chokes on the smoke*]
	It's no good. We can't go out that way.
Lisa	Why? What's up?
Pam	[*Still coughing*] The staircase is filled with smoke.
Lisa	Then what shall we do?
Pam	We'll get the sheets off the bed and tie them together and make a rope.
Lisa	What good will that do?
Pam	We'll tie it to the balcony and climb down it.
Lisa	Don't be stupid, Pam. It's a parachute we need. We're on the tenth floor.
Pam	I'd forgotten we were so high up. How about my umbrella?
Lisa	Not unless you're Mary Poppins in disguise. And I'm not risking it.
Pam	It is a long way down, isn't it? There's quite a crowd down there now, look.
Lisa	There's a man shouting something up to

us. What's he saying, Pam?

Pam   Stop your nattering and perhaps we'll be able to hear.

[*Off stage*]

Man   Throw the baby down.

Lisa   [*Coughing*] What's he say, Pam?

Pam   He says throw little Helen down.

Lisa   Throw her down? He's got to be joking.

Pam   Tell him then.

Lisa   [*Shouting down*] Get lost. I'm not throwing my baby down.

Man   She'll be all right. I'll catch her. I never fail.

Lisa   How do I know that? You could miss her.

Man   Never missed a catch yet – honest. I'm a goalkeeper.

Lisa   Well, I'm not sure. Who do you play for?

Man   United. I'm goalkeeper on the first team. She'll be in safe hands. Never miss a catch.

Pam   Oh go on, Lisa. What are you waiting for? Goalkeepers are great catchers. Go

8

	on. Throw her down. It's our only chance.
Lisa	Oh all right then – if you think so. Hey, mister, here she comes.
Man	Right. I'm ready.

[*Cries of falling* Baby]

Lisa	[*Screaming*] Oh no … oh no …
Pam	What happened? Didn't he catch her?
Lisa	Oh, he caught her all right. But then he bounced her twice on the ground and kicked her over the wall.

The Borrower

3 parts:
Arthur, his wife, *Ethel* and the next door neighbour, *Ted*

Scene A garden

Arthur Nice day, Ethel.

Ethel Lovely.

Arthur It's been a long time since we've had a day in the garden.

Ethel You're right, Arthur. It is a long time. I shall really enjoy myself today.

Arthur Well, don't speak too soon. We've got company. Ted's walking over to the fence.

Ethel Oh not that old scrounger. He'll want to borrow our lawnmower or something. Say we're using it. Don't let him borrow anything.

Arthur Right.

[Ted *looks over fence*]

Ted	Hello, Ethel. Hello, Arthur. You look busy.
Arthur	Yes, we are, Ted, very busy.
Ted	Nice day for a spot of gardening. Not too hot and not too cold.
Ethel	Yes, very nice.
Ted	I can see you're using your fork, Ethel. Nice fork that.
Ethel	Yes, you're right. It is a nice fork and I'm using it to dig this bed. And if you've come to ask if you can borrow it – you can't and I don't see why you can't buy your own.
Ted	Oh I would but I'm broke.
Ethel	Why are you broke?
Ted	I've just had to pay the dentist 100 pounds for taking out my tooth.
Arthur	Don't be daft. The dentist doesn't charge 100 pounds for taking out one tooth.
Ted	Well, mine did.
Ethel	Why?
Ted	I screamed so loud I frightened away all his other patients.
Arthur	Then you'll just have to get a job that pays better.

Ted	Can't do that. I never passed no exams when I was at school.
Arthur	Did you find them hard?
Ted	Half hard and half easy.
Ethel	How do you mean?
Ted	Well I found the questions easy – it was the answers I had difficulty with.
Arthur	Oh come on, Ethel. We can't stand around listening to Ted's daft stories.
Ethel	No. We've got work to do.
Ted	Are you going to dig that bed?
Arthur	I am.
Ted	That's a very nice spade you've got, Arthur. It's the one I borrowed last week, isn't it?
Arthur	Yes, it is.
Ted	The one our Elvis hit Shane over the head with.
Ethel	Oh dear. Was he badly hurt?
Ted	No, but he didn't half dent your spade.
Arthur	Well, I'm using it today. And Ethel's using the fork.

Ted	And are you mowing the lawn today, as well?
Arthur	Yes.
Ted	Then it's a good job I repaired your mower last week.
Ethel	But it wasn't broken.
Ted	It was after our Sandra ran it into the apple tree.
Arthur	Well we'll be using it today so there's no chance of you borrowing it again.
Ted	My goodness, you will be busy.
Ethel	We certainly will.
Ted	And are you going to water all your plants, as well?
Arthur	Yes, and that means we'll be using the hose pipe . . .
Ethel	. . . and the lawnmower and the fork and the spade.
Ted	What a busy pair.
Arthur	We'll even be using the hoe and the rake.
Ethel	Right. So you can't borrow them.
Ted	And the shears and the wheelbarrow?

Arthur	The fork, the spade, the lawnmower, the hose, the hoe, the rake, the shears and the wheelbarrow. We'll be that busy gardening we'll use everything we've got.
Ted	Everything?
Ethel	You've got it Ted.
Ted	Got it.
Arthur	You see it's like this, Ted – we are going to spend all day in the garden. We shall be working every minute of daylight.
Ethel	Every minute till it goes dark. Every minute.
Ted	Well, that's all right then.
Arthur	What do you mean – that's all right?
Ted	Well, if you're spending all day in the garden, you won't be needing your new cricket bat – so I'll be able to borrow it, won't I?

Trouble Sleeping

2 parts:

A husband and wife, *Alf* and *Edna*

Scene A bedroom. *Alf* and *Edna* are sitting up in bed.

Edna	I'm fed up.
Alf	Why's that, Edna?
Edna	Because I can't sleep.
Alf	Have you been falling out of bed again?
Edna	No, I haven't.
Alf	You fell out last week.
Edna	When?
Alf	Last Friday. Don't you remember?
Edna	No.
Alf	You put too much night cream on your face and you slid off the mattress.
Edna	Well, that's not why I can't sleep. I haven't been falling out of bed.

Alf	Have you been having that bad dream again?
Edna	What bad dream?
Alf	The one where you're drowning in a swimming pool.
Edna	When did I dream I was drowning in a swimming pool?
Alf	You remember – last Thursday night.
Edna	No.
Alf	Last Thursday night when your hot water bottle burst.
Edna	No, it's not that. I've not been having bad dreams.
Alf	Then what is it?
Edna	It's the noise.
Alf	But I thought you didn't mind them building a motorway at the bottom of the garden.
Edna	No, I didn't mind them building the motorway.
Alf	Then why is it keeping you awake?
Edna	It's not that noise that keeps me awake.
Alf	Then tell me.

Edna	Just every few minutes – it roars like thunder in my ears. Terrible it is.
Alf	Well if it's the planes taking off every hour, I suppose it is a bit hard to drop off.
Edna	No, it's not the planes and it's not the motorway.
Alf	Then what is it?
Edna	It's your snoring, Alf.
Alf	My snoring?
Edna	Your snoring. It's driving me mad.
Alf	Oh.
Edna	You lie there and you snore right in my ear.
Alf	Well, I've tried putting a peg on my nose.
Edna	And it didn't work.
Alf	And I slept with a sock in my mouth.
Edna	And that didn't work either.
Alf	Well I don't know what I can do to stop it.
Edna	We'll have to think of something.
Alf	We'll have to.
Edna	Why don't you try the floor.

Alf	The floor?
Edna	Try sleeping on the floor.
Alf	Will that stop it?
Edna	Well if it doesn't stop you snoring at least you won't be snoring in my ear, will you?
Alf	No, I suppose I won't.
Edna	Then will you try it?
Alf	All right. I'll have a go.
Edna	Good.
Alf	Anything for a bit of peace and quiet.
Edna	Right then. Go and lie down over there.
Alf	Where?
Edna	Over there by the wall.
Alf	You mean right over the other side of the room?
Edna	That's it.
Alf	Right you are.
Edna	You lie down. I'll bring your things.
Alf	Right, Edna.
Edna	Here you are. Here's your pillow.
Alf	Thanks.

Edna	And put this blanket over you.
Alf	Thanks. That should be warm enough.
Edna	Right. That's you settled. I'll get back to bed.
Alf	It's a bit hard is this floor, Edna.
Edna	You'll be all right.
Alf	Don't know if I'll be able to sleep here.
Edna	Of course you will, Alf. You could sleep on a washing line.
Alf	I hope you're right.
Edna	Course I am. Goodnight, duck.
Alf	Goodnight, Edna.
	[Alf *snores*] Help!...Help...
Edna	What's the matter?
Alf	I'm dying...Help.
Edna	What do you mean – you're dying?
Alf	Something's just run down my throat.
Edna	Are you sure?
Alf	Of course I'm sure. It was something with four legs. I felt it.
Edna	Something with four legs running down your

throat? What could it be?

Alf	It must be that mouse we've been trying to catch all week.
Edna	It could be.
Alf	But why did he run down my throat?
Edna	Because you always sleep with your mouth open.
Alf	What's that got to do with it?
Edna	He must have thought your mouth was a mouse hole.
Alf	What shall I do?
Edna	I don't know.
Alf	Well, think of something quick.
Edna	I've got an idea.
Alf	What?
Edna	I'll get the cheese out of the trap and I'll tie it to the end of your nose.
Alf	What good's that?
Edna	The mouse will smell the cheese.
Alf	So what? I don't get it.
Edna	The mouse will smell the cheese and he'll come out to get it.

Alf	Oh now I see. Good idea, Edna. Good idea.
Edna	I'll go and get the cheese, shall I?
Alf	You do that. I'll stay put.

[Edna *goes out and comes back with cheese and string*]

Edna	Here we are.
Alf	Good. Did you get some string as well?
Edna	Yes, here's the string.
Alf	Great.
Edna	I'll tie it nice and tight.

[Edna *ties cheese to* Alf's *nose*]

Alf	A bit painful, Edna.
Edna	Well, never mind. Just as long as it does the trick.
Alf	Hope my nose doesn't fall off.
Edna	It's not that tight, Alf. Now you go back to sleep.
Alf	OK, I'll try, Edna.

[Alf *snores*] Help . . . . . . help.

Edna	What is it? Has the mouse come up after the cheese?
Alf	No.
Edna	Then what?
Alf	The cat's gone in after the mouse – HELP . . .

A New Carpet

3 parts:
A housewife, *Mrs Jackson*, two carpet fitters, *Terry* and *Frank*

Scene Inside a house.

Terry	Good afternoon, Madam. Are you Mrs Jackson?
Mrs J	Yes, I am.
Terry	Well, I'm Terry and this is my mate, Frank, and we've come to fit your new carpet.
Mrs J	Bring it into the kitchen, will you and close the door.
Terry	Thanks.
Frank	Yeh, thanks.
Mrs J	You're very late. You were supposed to come at nine this morning. It's three o'clock now.
Terry	Ah yes. Sorry about that. We had a small problem, didn't we, Frank?

Frank	That's right, Terry. A small problem.
Mrs J	And what was this small problem?
Terry	I lost the keys to the van.
Mrs J	You lost the keys?
Terry	Yeh.
Mrs J	And how long did it take you to find them?
Terry	About ten minutes. That's right, isn't it Frank?
Frank	Yeh, that's right, Terry, about ten minutes.
Mrs J	If it only took you ten minutes to find the keys then why are you six hours late?
Terry	We had another problem.
Mrs J	Another one?
Terry	Yeh, we had another one, didn't we, Frank?
Frank	We did, Terry – another problem.
Mrs J	Tell me.
Terry	Well, we were going along the motorway happy as larks ... the sun was shining and we were looking forward to laying your carpet ...
Mrs J	What happened?
Terry	Well, my mate Frank here was doing the

map reading – you love map reading don't you, Frank?

Frank   That's right, Terry, I do. I love map reading.

Mrs J   Go on ... Go on.

Terry   Well, it was about ten o'clock and I looked down at the map in Frank's hands.

Mrs J   Well?

Terry   He'd got it up-side-down hadn't he? We were going north instead of south.

Frank   That's right, we were, lady. We were going north.

Mrs J   I don't believe it.

Terry   True as I stand in this kitchen. Mind if I smoke?

Mrs J   No, that's all right.

Terry   I like a fag when I've had a hard day. But not to worry. Everything's OK now. After we changed the wheel, we came right here.

Mrs J   Changed the wheel?

Terry   When we had the flat tyre.

Frank   Yeh – a flat tyre.

Mrs J   I think you're making this up. I don't

believe a word of it.

Terry	It's the truth, honest.
Frank	Yeh, honest.
Terry	Tell you what – just to make up for being so late, Mrs Jackson, we'll lay your carpet fast – really fast.
Frank	Yeh, really fast.
Mrs J	How fast's that?
Terry	We'll lay it in the time it takes you to make us a cup of tea.
Mrs J	Never.
Terry	We'll show you.
Mrs J	I don't believe it.
Terry	You'll see. Come on, Frank. You take one end of the carpet and I'll take the other.
Frank	Right, Terry.
Terry	This way, is it, Mrs Jackson?
Mrs J	Yes, right across the hall.
Terry	Right you are.
Frank	Right you are.

[*There is a good deal of banging as the men lay the carpet*]

Terry	Well, we've done it again, Frank. Pretty fast work, eh?
Frank	Yeh, we've done it again, Terry.
Terry	Looks good, doesn't it?
Frank	Yes ... but ...
Terry	But what?
Frank	There's a lump, Terry.
Terry	Where?
Frank	Right there.
Terry	Where?
Frank	In the middle, Terry.
Terry	Oh no. It's my cigarettes. I must have left them on the floor.
Frank	Are we going to take the carpet up again, Terry?
Terry	No. It would take too long. Anyway, there's no need for that. I'll flatten it with my hammer. Mrs Jackson will never notice.
	[*There is the sound of banging*]
Mrs J	Well, well, well ... I see you've finished the carpet. That was quick – very quick. And here's your tea nice and hot.

27

Terry	Thanks.
Frank	Yeh, thanks.
Mrs J	And here's your cigarettes. You left them in the kitchen. I expect you're ready for a smoke.
Terry	C-c-c-cigarettes??
Mrs J	Yes, here they are. And, by the way ... you haven't seen the hamster have you? I left the cage door open and he got out.

No School Today

2 parts:
David and *Wendy*

Scene A bedroom

Wendy	David, are you awake yet?
David	No.
Wendy	Don't be silly. I know you're awake.
David	I'm not. I'm asleep and I'm staying asleep.
Wendy	I've called you three times. Now get up.
David	No.
Wendy	Well, if you want to be late for school, that's up to you.
David	I don't care.
Wendy	Of course you care.
David	Don't.
Wendy	Oh, come on, David. Don't be silly. Get up.
David	I'm not getting up.

Wendy	Yes you are.
David	I'm not getting up. I'm staying in bed.
Wendy	David, you can't stay in bed.
David	Why not?
Wendy	Because you've got to go to school.
David	Why?
Wendy	Because the teachers will be mad with you, if you don't go.
David	Well I get mad with them when I do go. They'll be glad I stayed at home.
Wendy	Come on, David. This isn't like you.
David	Yes it is like me.
Wendy	I don't know what to say.
David	Don't bother to say anything. I'm not getting up.
Wendy	Look, love, I've put a nice clean shirt and tie out for you. Come on, get up.
David	No. Leave me alone.
Wendy	Well, shall I bring you a nice cup of tea?
David	No. I just want to stay in bed.
Wendy	What's the matter, David?
David	Nothing.

30

Wendy	There must be something. Go on, tell me.
David	I'm fed up.
Wendy	Oh.
David	Very fed up.
Wendy	What are you fed up about?
David	It's the kids.
Wendy	The kids?
David	The kids at school.
Wendy	Yes.
David	They keep picking on me.
Wendy	How do they do that?
David	Last week they put chewing gum on my chair.
Wendy	They didn't. *did they*
David	They did. *yes*
Wendy	Go on.
David	And they put a mouse in my desk, too.
Wendy	Oh, that must have made you jump.
David	It did.
Wendy	Yes.
David	I nearly jumped out of my skin.

Wendy	What else do they do, David?
David	They laugh at me.
Wendy	Do they?
David	All the time they laugh at me.
Wendy	Go on.
David	They laugh at the way I dress.
Wendy	No.
David	They say my clothes are old fashioned.
Wendy	But you always wear a nice clean shirt and tie.
David	But they don't wear shirts and ties.
Wendy	Don't they?
David	No, they wear tee shirts and jeans.
Wendy	Well, you can't wear jeans. Not for school.
David	I know.
Wendy	What else do they do?
David	They call me names.
Wendy	What sort of names?
David	They call me 'bird brain'.
Wendy	When?

David	In the science lessons. When my experiments go wrong.
Wendy	Oh, if I could lay my hands on the little horrors.
David	But that's not all ...
Wendy	Go on, David, tell me.
David	It's the computer.
Wendy	Computer?
David	Yes. I don't understand the computer.
Wendy	Oh.
David	They laugh at me because I don't know how to use it.
Wendy	But, David, you're quite clever.
David	I still don't understand computers like they do.
Wendy	And so they laugh at you?
David	Yes.
Wendy	And ... ?
David	They laugh at my spelling, too.
Wendy	Your spelling?
David	Yes. Sometimes I make mistakes.

Wendy	Oh, David.
David	Then they throw things at me.
Wendy	What things?
David	All sorts of things. Chewing gum, paper darts ...
Wendy	Disgusting.
David	And there's cricket, too.
Wendy	How do you mean?
David	When we have a game of cricket, they laugh.
Wendy	Why's that?
David	Because I can't run as fast as they can.
Wendy	Shame.
David	They laugh when I bowl and I miss the wicket.
Wendy	Well I never.
David	All the time they laugh.
Wendy	They do, don't they?
David	So now you see.
Wendy	See what?
David	Why I don't want to go to school.

Wendy	Yes, I do see, David.
David	Good. Then I'm going back to sleep.
Wendy	No, you're not.
David	Oh.
Wendy	You still have to go.
David	I don't see why.
Wendy	Well, I do – you're the headmaster.

The Fortune Teller

2 parts:
Fortune teller, Stella

Scene A fortune teller's tent.

Fortune teller Come in, dear. Sit down.

Stella Thank you.

Fortune teller Now – what can I do for you?

Stella I want to see into the future.

Fortune teller Ah yes ... very well. Everybody wants to see into the future. Yes. I'm sure. Right then – but first of all, let me get my pencil.

Stella Why do you need a pencil?

Fortune teller I need it for the numbers.

Stella The numbers?

Fortune teller Yes, I want you to say ten numbers.

Stella Any ten?

Fortune teller Ten numbers between 1 and 55.

Stella	Right then . . . 3 . . . 6 . . . 9 . . . 11 . . . 14
Fortune teller	Ooooh, that's interesting. Go on.
Stella	. . . 18 . . . 21 . . . 34 . . .
Fortune teller	Yes, just another two.
Stella	36 . . . 39.
Fortune teller	I knew it – Manchester and Newcastle. Very good – very good.
Stella	Do the numbers say that I'll be going there?
Fortune teller	The numbers? Oh, I see what you mean, dear. Good gracious me, no. I was just doing the football pools.
Stella	Have you been a fortune teller long?
Fortune teller	No dear. I used to be a singer but I got a frog in my throat.
Stella	So you couldn't sing any more.
Fortune teller	No, it wasn't that. My agent said the frog sounded better than I did. Very upsetting.
Stella	It must have been.
Fortune teller	Now then, shall I look into my crystal ball or shall I read your palm?
Stella	Crystal ball, I think.

37

Fortune teller	Right you are, then. That'll be 50 pence.
Stella	Here you are. Now let's see what's in your crystal ball.
Fortune teller	Ahhhhhhhhh ...
Stella	What is it?
Fortune teller	I can see a mist.
Stella	Just a mist? Nothing else?
Fortune teller	Wait a minute. I'll get a clean cloth. Yes, that's better. I haven't used the ball for a week or two. Things get so dusty, don't they? Now then, what can I see? Ahhhhhhh ...
Stella	Yes? What is it?
Fortune teller	I can see ... I can see a far away country. Far, far across the sea.
Stella	Where is it?
Fortune teller	It's Africa. You will travel to Africa – yes, I can see it clearly.
Stella	Show me.
Fortune teller	Here, look.
Stella	I think if you lift up your crystal ball you'll see that Africa is just a tea stain on the cloth.

Fortune teller	Ah yes, well never mind. Let's take another look.
Stella	Yes ... now what can you see?
Fortune teller	I can see you in the ball.
Stella	Can you?
Fortune teller	Yes, I can see you with a man.
Stella	What's he like?
Fortune teller	He's thin and he has dark hair.
Stella	Yes.
Fortune teller	He has dark hair and glasses.
Stella	Yes.
Fortune teller	He has dark hair and glasses and a big nose.
Stella	Yes.
Fortune teller	The man is your husband ...
Stella	Yes ... yes ... that's spot on. Very good. You got it right. That's Fred.
Fortune teller	... and I see a house ... a small house ...
Stella	Yes.
Fortune teller	... with a blue and white kitchen.
Stella	Oh yes, that's my kitchen. Ever so nice

it is. What else can you see?

Fortune teller   What else? Nothing else. Do you expect miracles for 50 pence?

Stella   But I want to see into the future.

Fortune teller   Then it'll cost you.

Stella   How much?

Fortune teller   A quid.

Stella   A pound? You must be joking.

Fortune teller   You've got to pay for talent these days, you know.

Stella   Oh, all right then. Here's your pound. But I want to see what's going to happen, this time.

Fortune teller   Right then. Let's have another go. Let's see if we can look into the future .... Ah yes.

Stella   What is it? What can you see?

Fortune teller   I can see that man again.

Stella   Yes.

Fortune teller   The man with dark hair and glasses and big nose.

Stella   We've done all that before.

Fortune teller	No, no. This time he's lying on the floor.
Stella	Yes.
Fortune teller	He's lying on the floor in the blue and white kitchen.
Stella	Yes.
Fortune teller	I can see blood. A lot of blood.
Stella	Yes.
Fortune teller	There is a knife sticking in the man's back ...
Stella	Yes.
Fortune teller	and there is blood everywhere ... on the floor ... on the walls ... everywhere.
Stella	Yes.
Fortune teller	You don't sound surprised.
Stella	No, I'm not. I know all about that.
Fortune teller	Then why did you need a fortune teller?
Stella	It's simple. I want to know if I'll get found out.

Hutchinson Education
An imprint of Century Hutchinson Ltd
62-65 Chandos Place
London WC2N 4NW

Century Hutchinson Australia Pty Ltd
89-91 Albion Street, Surry Hills,
New South Wales 2010, Australia

Century Hutchinson New Zealand Limited
PO Box 40-086, Glenfield, Auckland 10,
New Zealand

Century Hutchinson South Africa (Pty) Ltd
PO Box 337, Bergvlei 2012, South Africa

First published 1986
Reprinted 1989
© Barbara Mitchelhill 1986

Set in Linotron 202 Rockwell

Printed and bound in Great Britain

British Library Cataloguing in Publication Data

Mitchelhill, Barbara
    Punchlines. – (Spirals)
    1. Readers – 1950-
    I. Title   II. Series
    428.6'2   PE1119
ISBN 0 09 163461 X